WITHDRAWN

DATE DUE

2/27/06

MAR 2 8 2006	
APR 2 1 2006	
MAY 1 7 2006	
JUN 0 3 2006	
JUN 1 2 2006	
SEP 2 9 2006	
JAN 1 0 2007	
MAR 1 6 2007	

To the Extreme

Paintball

by Mandy R. Marx

Reading Consultant:
Barbara J. Fox
Reading Specialist
North Carolina State University

Capstone press

Mankato, Minnesota

Blazers is published by Capstone Press,
151 Good Counsel Drive, P.O. Box 669, Mankato, Minnesota 56002.
www.capstonepress.com

Library of Congress Cataloging-in-Publication Data
Marx, Mandy R.
   Paintball / by Mandy R. Marx.
   p. cm.—(Blazers. To the extreme)
   Includes bibliographical references and index.
   ISBN-13: 978-0-7368-5463-4 (hardcover)
   ISBN-10: 0-7368-5463-0 (hardcover)
   1. Paintball (Game)—Juvenile literature. I. Title. II. Series.
GV1202.S87 M37 2006
796.2—dc22   2005020089

Summary: Describes the sport of paintball, including gear, safety
   equipment, and competitions.

Editorial Credits
Carrie A. Braulick, editor; Jason Knudson, set designer; Kate Opseth
   and Jennifer Bergstrom, book designers; Wanda Winch, photo
   researcher; Scott Thoms, photo editor

Photo Credits
Capstone Press/Karon Dubke, cover, 5, 6, 7, 8, 11, 12, 15, 16–17, 28–29
Getty Images Inc./Stone/Sean Murphy, 19; Tim Boyle, 27
Steve Lashbrook, official photographer of the NPPL Super 7 World
   Series, 20, 23, 24, 25

The publisher does not endorse products whose logos may appear on
objects in images in this book.

**Capstone Press thanks Tommygun's Paint Wars, New Ulm, Minn., for
their assistance with this book.**

1 2 3 4 5 6 11 10 09 08 07 06

Table of Contents

Capture the Flag

In a wooded area, a man in camouflage crouches behind a tree. He spots the orange enemy flag close by.

The player creeps up to the flag. A sniper on the other team spots him. Splat! A paintball hits a tree near his head.

It was a close call, but the player is safe. He snatches the flag and races to his team's flag station. His team claims victory.

BLAZER FACT

Capture the flag is a popular paintball game. Players must take the other team's flag and bring it to their own flag station without being hit.

Paintball Gear

Paintball players need the right gear. Paintball guns are the most important tools. These guns are called markers.

Hopper

Players pour paintballs into a hopper on top of the marker. About 200 paintballs fit into a hopper.

BLAZER FACT

Paintballs don't actually contain paint. They hold a colored liquid that easily washes off with soap and water.

Markers also have air tanks and triggers. A player pulls the trigger to release pressure in the air tank. A paintball then speeds toward its target.

BLAZER FACT

A paintball fired from a gun can travel up to 300 feet (91 meters) per second.

Trigger

Air tank

Paintball Diagram

Marker

Air tank

Face mask

Hopper

Gloves

A Safe Sport

Safety gear makes paintball one of the safest sports around. It is safer than golf, tennis, and bicycling.

Players wear face masks to protect their faces and necks. Wearing gloves, long-sleeved shirts, and pants is also a good idea.

BLAZER FACT

When paintball first began, players didn't have the right safety gear. They wore ski or welding goggles to protect their eyes.

Get in the Game

Paintball has grown since it started in 1981. What began as a game between friends is now a professional sport.

Professional paintball is called speedball. Pro players compete in the National XBall League.

Pro paintball is popular, but most people play just for fun. Amateurs can rent gear at most paintball fields to get in on the action.

BLAZER FACT

The International Amateur Open is one of the largest events for amateur players. It is held in Pennsylvania each year.

Caught in a trap!

Glossary

amateur (AM-uh-chur)—an athlete who does not earn a living from competing in a sport

camouflage (KAM-uh-flahzh)—coloring or covering that makes animals, people, and objects blend in with their surroundings

goggles (GOG-uhlz)—protective glasses that fit tightly around the eyes

hopper (HOP-uhr)—the container on a paintball gun that holds the paintballs

marker (MAHR-kuhr)—a paintball gun

sniper (SNY-puhr)—a paintball player who shoots at other players from a hiding place

Read More

Davidson, Steve, et al. *The Complete Guide to Paintball.* Long Island City, N.Y.: Hatherleigh Press, 2004.

Little, John R., and Curtis F. Wong, eds. *Ultimate Guide to Paintball.* Lincolnwood, Ill.: Contemporary Books, 2001.

Sievert, Terri. *Paintball.* Edge Books. X-Sports. Mankato, Minn.: Capstone Press, 2005.

Internet Sites

FactHound offers a safe, fun way to find Internet sites related to this book. All of the sites on FactHound have been researched by our staff.

Here's how:

1. Visit *www.facthound.com*
2. Type in this special code **0736854630** for age-appropriate sites. Or, enter a search word related to this book for a more general search.
3. Click on the **Fetch It** button.

FactHound will fetch the best sites for you!

Index